Before They Were President

BEFORE THOMAS JEFFERSON WAS PRESIDENT

By Michael Rajczak

Gareth Stevens
PUBLISHING

Please visit our website, www.garethstevens.com. For a free color catalog of all our high-quality books, call toll free 1-800-542-2595 or fax 1-877-542-2596.

Library of Congress Cataloging-in-Publication Data

Names: Rajczak, Michael, author.
Title: Before Thomas Jefferson was President / Michael Rajczak.
Description: New York : Gareth Stevens Publishing, [2019] | Series: Before they were president | Includes index.
Identifiers: LCCN 2018023955| ISBN 9781538229132 (library bound) | ISBN 9781538232569 (paperback) | ISBN 9781538232576 (6 pack)
Subjects: LCSH: Jefferson, Thomas, 1743-1826–Juvenile literature. | Presidents–United States–Biography–Juvenile literature. | LCGFT: Biographies.
Classification: LCC E332.79 .R34 2019 | DDC 973.4/6092 [B] –dc23
LC record available at https://lccn.loc.gov/2018023955

First Edition

Published in 2019 by
Gareth Stevens Publishing
111 East 14th Street, Suite 349
New York, NY 10003

Copyright © 2019 Gareth Stevens Publishing

Designer: Laura Bowen
Editor: Therese Shea

Photo credits: Cover, p. 1 (Jefferson) John Parrot/Stocktrek Images/Getty Images; cover, p. 1 (background) UniversalImagesGroup/Getty Images; cover, pp. 1–21 (frame) Samran wonglakorn/Shutterstock.com; p. 5 (inset) Zainubrazvi-commonswiki/Wikimedia Commons; p. 7 James Shelton32/Wikimedia Commons; p. 9 Joshua Reynolds/Jalo/Wikimedia Commons; p. 11 Jeff Greenberg/Universal Images Group/Getty Images; p. 13 (main) jiawangkun/Shutterstock.com; p. 13 (inset) Everett Historical/Shutterstock.com; p. 15 Bruce Ellis/Shutterstock.com; p. 17 (main) Parhamr/Wikimedia Commons; p. 17 (inset) John Trumbull/Cmdrjameson/Wikimedia Commons; p. 19 (main) Joe Ravi/Jovianeye/Wikimedia Commons; p. 19 (inset) Thomas Sully/Freaktheclown/Wikimedia Commons; p. 21 (top) BrianPlrwin/Shutterstock.com; p. 21 (bottom) Rembrandt Peale/Ibn Battuta/Wikimedia Commons.

Printed in the United States of America

CPSIA compliance information: Batch #CW19GS: For further information contact Gareth Stevens, New York, New York at 1-800-542-2595.

CONTENTS

Words in the glossary appear in **bold** type the first time they are used in the text.

TWO HOMES

Thomas Jefferson was born on April 13, 1743, at Shadwell, a **plantation** in Virginia. His father, Peter Jefferson, was a successful **tobacco** planter. Not much is known about his mother, Jane Randolph. Thomas was the third of their 10 children and the oldest boy.

After the death of Jane's cousin William Randolph, the Jefferson family moved to Tuckahoe Plantation to care for the Randolph children. Thomas's earliest memory was riding horseback to Tuckahoe in the arms of a slave when he was 2 or 3 years old.

Presidential Preview

Peter Jefferson held many jobs in his life, just as his son Thomas would. Besides being a tobacco farmer, Peter had been a **justice of the peace**, sheriff, and **surveyor**.

BLUE RIDGE MOUNTAINS

Thomas Jefferson's first home, Shadwell, was located on the Rivanna River in the hills of the Blue Ridge Mountains.

MD

WV

Shadwell

Tuckahoe

VA

KY

TN

NC

5

TIME AT TUCKAHOE

Peter Jefferson didn't have much schooling, but he taught himself by reading. It was important to him that his children receive a good education. He hired a teacher for the one-room schoolhouse at Tuckahoe.

At the age of 5, Thomas joined the other children learning to read and write. When he was 9, the Jefferson family moved back to Shadwell. Peter arranged for Thomas to continue his education at the school of Reverend William Douglas.

Presidential Preview

Thomas Jefferson wrote that Reverend Douglas knew little Latin and Greek, but said Douglas taught him French. Jefferson would use his knowledge of French when he became US **minister** to France.

THOMAS JEFFERSON SPENT MUCH OF HIS BOYHOOD AT TUCKAHOE PLANTATION. SOME OF THE HOUSE'S DESIGNS WERE USED IN THE DESIGNS FOR MONTICELLO, THE HOME HE LATER BUILT.

HOME AND SCHOOL

Thomas Jefferson lived at Reverend Douglas's school, but went home to Shadwell from time to time. Sometimes there were exciting visitors to Shadwell. For example, Cherokee chief Ostenaco (whom Jefferson called Outassete) would visit on his way to and from Williamsburg, the capital of Virginia. Young Thomas was a welcomed guest in their camp.

After Peter Jefferson's death in 1757, Thomas studied with Reverend James Maury for 2 years. He learned about languages, books, and science. He said those years were some of the happiest of his life.

Presidential Preview

Thomas Jefferson practiced the violin up to 3 hours a day. He called music "the favorite passion of my soul."

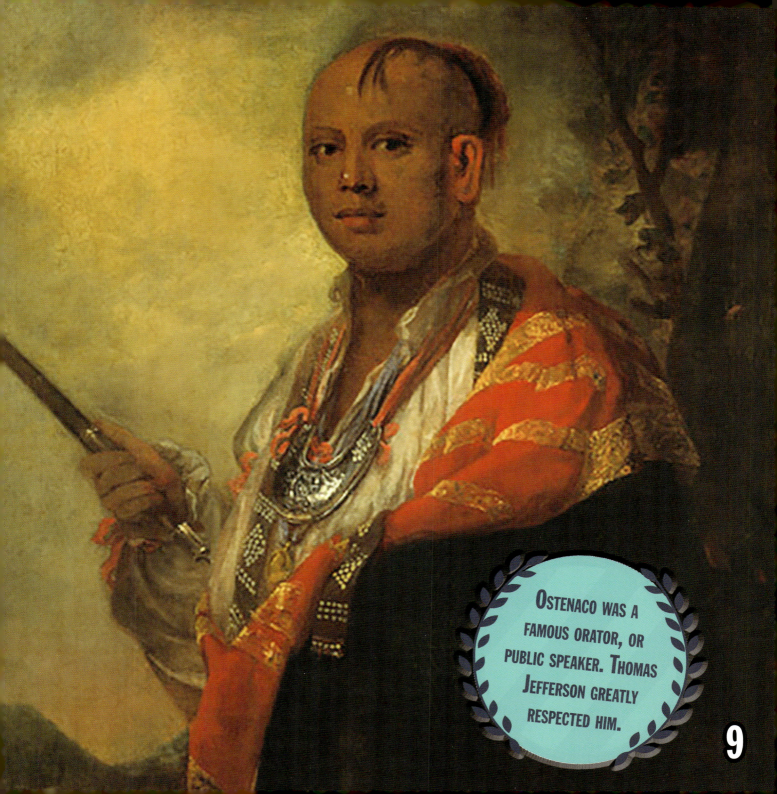

OSTENACO WAS A FAMOUS ORATOR, OR PUBLIC SPEAKER. THOMAS JEFFERSON GREATLY RESPECTED HIM.

9

TALL TOM

Thomas Jefferson grew tall. By the time the red-headed, freckled boy was a teenager, his friends called him "Tall Tom."

Jefferson believed his "whole care and direction" was his own responsibility after his father's death. Some of the people he surrounded himself with weren't good role models. Luckily, he also knew people of good character. He found himself wishing to be like them. He later said he would ask himself what he wished his **reputation** to be. Jefferson thought this helped him stay on the right path.

Presidential Preview

Throughout his life, Jefferson took long rides on horseback to be alone and think. He was a skilled horseback rider.

THOMAS JEFFERSON LOVED READING. HE SOLD MORE THAN 6,000 OF HIS BOOKS TO THE LIBRARY OF CONGRESS. VISITORS TO THE LIBRARY OF CONGRESS CAN LOOK AT JEFFERSON'S COLLECTION.

WILLIAMSBURG

In 1760, Thomas Jefferson went to the College of William and Mary in Williamsburg. Two years later, when he was 19, Jefferson became an **apprentice** to lawyer George Wythe. There were no law schools, so law students learned by working with practicing lawyers. Jefferson became a lawyer in 1767.

In 1768, Jefferson was elected to the Virginia legislature, or lawmaking body, which was called the House of Burgesses. At that time, the American colonies were still under British rule. Jefferson heard many arguments about whether the colonies should free themselves.

Presidential Preview

It's said that Jefferson studied for up to 15 hours a day in college.

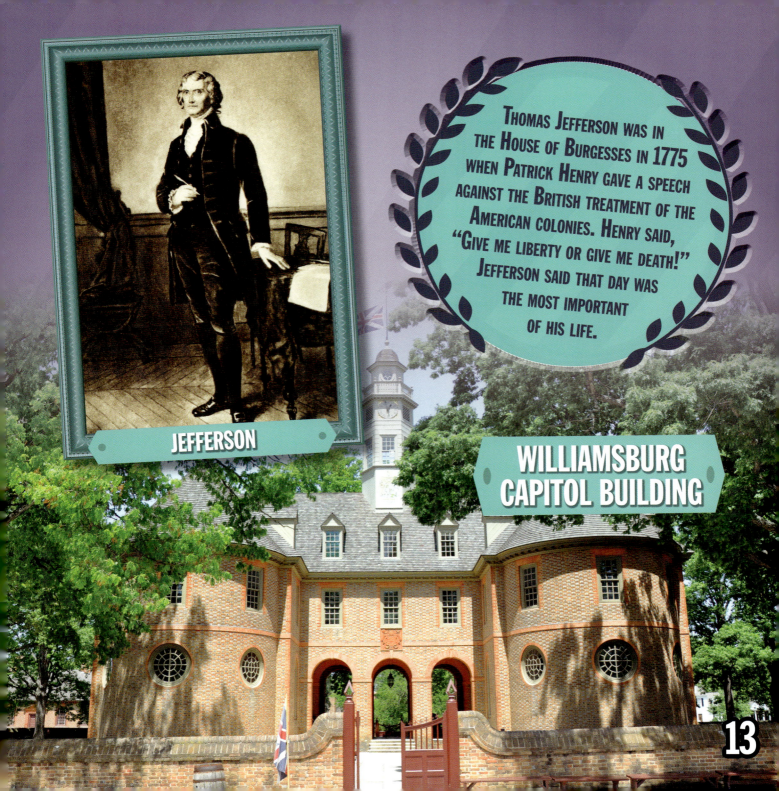

JEFFERSON

Thomas Jefferson was in the House of Burgesses in 1775 when Patrick Henry gave a speech against the British treatment of the American colonies. Henry said, "Give me liberty or give me death!" Jefferson said that day was the most important of his life.

WILLIAMSBURG CAPITOL BUILDING

MONTICELLO

After his father's death, Jefferson received land. He always dreamed of building a house on it. In 1768, he began to level the top of a small mountain. The house he built there is called Monticello, which means "little mountain" in Italian.

In 1772, Jefferson married Martha Wayles Skelton. He brought her to Monticello although it wasn't completed. It took more than 10 years to build this house. But when Jefferson's ideas about its design changed, most of it was torn down and a new building was constructed. Monticello was finally completed in 1809.

Presidential Preview

Jefferson owned more than 600 slaves throughout his lifetime. However, later in his life he argued against slavery and tried to have it outlawed.

THE CLAY BRICKS FOR MONTICELLO WERE FORMED AND BAKED ON THE PROPERTY. MOST OF THE CLAY, LUMBER, AND STONE THAT WAS USED IN CONSTRUCTION CAME FROM THIS LAND, TOO. JEFFERSON EVEN HAD THE NAILS MADE ON SITE.

A TALENT FOR WRITING

In 1774, a meeting called the Continental Congress took place in Philadelphia, Pennsylvania. Jefferson wrote notes about the American colonies' rights for the Virginia **delegates**. His notes were printed for the public as *A Summary View of the Rights of British America*. People respected Jefferson's writing style.

After the **American Revolution** began in 1775, Jefferson became a delegate to the Second Continental Congress. The colonies wanted to state their independence. Jefferson was chosen to write the first **draft** of the Declaration of Independence.

Presidential Preview

Future president John Adams was one of the Committee of Five, the group in charge of writing the Declaration of Independence. He said Jefferson should write the first draft because "you can write ten times better than I can."

The unanimous Declaration of the thirteen united States of America.

COMMITTEE OF FIVE

IN THE DECLARATION OF INDEPENDENCE, JEFFERSON STATED THAT ALL PEOPLE HAVE THE RIGHT TO "LIFE, LIBERTY AND THE PURSUIT OF HAPPINESS." THESE WORDS EXPLAIN WHAT IT MEANS TO BE AN AMERICAN CITIZEN.

SERVING THE NEW NATION

Thomas Jefferson returned to Virginia in 1776 and was elected to the Virginia House of Delegates. He was governor of Virginia from 1779 to 1781.

In 1783, the American Revolution ended. The United States had won its independence. Jefferson served in what was called the Congress of the Confederation from 1783 to 1784.

In 1784, Jefferson traveled to France to be the US minister there. When he returned to the United States in 1790, he accepted the job of **secretary of state** from President George Washington.

Presidential Preview

Thomas Jefferson wrote the Virginia Statute for Establishing Religious Freedom in 1777. He thought it was one of his finest works. Part of this work is quoted inside the Jefferson Memorial in Washington, DC.

In 1782, Martha Jefferson died a few months after giving birth to a daughter. Jefferson never remarried. Only two of Martha and Thomas's six children lived to become adults.

THOMAS'S DAUGHTER, MARTHA "PATSY" JEFFERSON

THE THIRD PRESIDENT

Thomas Jefferson first ran for president in 1796. He came in second to John Adams, which meant he would become vice president. Jefferson and Adams disagreed about how to run the country. Jefferson was against the federal, or central, government gaining too much power.

In 1800, Jefferson ran for president again. This time, the election was a tie between Jefferson and Aaron Burr. The House of Representatives voted for Jefferson. Thomas Jefferson was sworn in as the third US president on March 4, 1801.

Presidential Preview

Thomas Jefferson was the president when the United States bought the Louisiana Territory from France in 1803. This land doubled the size of the United States.

Jefferson's Road to the Presidency

1743 — Thomas Jefferson is born April 13 at Shadwell Plantation in Virginia.

1760 — He begins at the College of William and Mary.

1767 — He becomes a lawyer.

1768 — He's elected to the House of Burgesses.

1774 — He writes *A Summary View of the Rights of British America*.

1775 — He's a delegate in the Second Continental Congress. He's chosen to write the Declaration of Independence.

1776 — He's elected to the Virginia House of Delegates.

1779 — He begins a term as the governor of Virginia.

1783 — He begins a term in the Congress of the Confederation.

1784 — He becomes the US minister to France.

1790 — He becomes the US secretary of state.

1796 — He's elected vice president.

1800 — He's elected the third president of the United States.

INSIDE JEFFERSON MEMORIAL

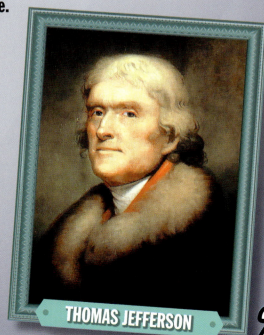

THOMAS JEFFERSON

GLOSSARY

American Revolution: the war in which the colonies won their freedom from England

apprentice: someone who learns a trade by working with a skilled person of that trade

delegate: a representative of one of the 13 colonies

design: the pattern or shape of something

draft: a piece of writing before completion

justice of the peace: a local official who has the power to decide minor legal cases

minister: an official who heads a government department or a major section of a department in some countries, such as Britain

plantation: a large farm

reputation: the views that are held about something or someone

secretary of state: the head of the US government department that is in charge of how the country relates to and deals with other countries

surveyor: one whose job is to measure land areas

tobacco: a plant that produces leaves that can be smoked or chewed

FOR MORE INFORMATION

Books

Bennett, Doraine. *Thomas Jefferson*. New York, NY: AV2 by Weigl, 2018.

Kalman, Maira. *Thomas Jefferson: Life, Liberty and the Pursuit of Everything*. New York, NY: Nancy Paulsen Books, 2014.

Websites

Biography: President Thomas Jefferson
www.ducksters.com/biography/uspresidents/thomasjefferson.php
Check out some quick facts about the third US president.

Thomas Jefferson
www.whitehouse.gov/about-the-white-house/presidents/thomas-jefferson/
Read a short biography of this president on the White House's website.

Thomas Jefferson's Monticello
home.monticello.org/
Take an online visit to Monticello, Thomas Jefferson's home.

INDEX